The Children and Jesus

By Cristina Marques

SCANDINAVIA

INTRODUCTION

Jesus said, "Become like little children." The Children of the Bible series puts attention on the littlest of Jesus' flock. Each of these characters has an inspiring story to tell. God used their lives to teach the world about his love. As you read these stories aloud, remember God's presence inside every child's spirit. The simplest stories sometimes hold the greatest power. May these stories be the beginning of a lifelong love of the Bible for your children. There is treasure to gain for young and old alike.

Jesus said, "Let the little children come to me and do not hinder them, for the kingdom of God belongs to such as these."

When Jesus was alive on earth, he loved to be with children! He blessed them and played with them. Jesus admired their pure hearts. His arms were always open for them.

Jesus taught children to love one another. We can please him by loving our parents. We can please him by loving our brothers and sisters. The more we love, the more we please God.

Jesus was a storyteller. One time he told a story about a farmer planting seeds. Some seeds fell onto rocky ground. These seeds didn't grow. Other seeds fell onto good soil. They grew big and tall. God's word is like a seed. It will grow inside a good heart.

Children are special to Jesus because they all belong to God. The Bible tells us that Jesus is our shepherd. We are his flock! If one of his little sheep is lost, Jesus will go out to find the lost one.

Praying is one of the best ways to feel close to Jesus. We can tell him anything! We can ask God to bless us. Sometimes the best prayers are when we ask God to bless others.

When we pray with an open heart, Jesus is listening. We may not see him with our eyes. We may not hear him with our ears. But we can know he is with us. Jesus lives inside our hearts.

Jesus doesn't want us to worry. "Look at the birds and butterflies," he said. "They don't worry because God takes care of them." God takes care of us, too. Share your joy with others, and you'll share the joy of Jesus.

Jesus loves us. Share his love with others. The more we love each other, the more we become like Jesus.

THE CHILDREN AND JESUS - LOVE

Jesus wants to be a part of our lives. He loves us! In his time, Jesus opened his arms to children. Today, we can still run to Jesus. We can pray. We can read the Bible. We can go to church. We can love each other. We can tell people about Jesus. Each time we do one of these things, it is like giving Jesus a hug. We can be close to him simply by loving people around us. Jesus' life is about love. Share this love with others!

© Scandinavia Publishing House
Drejervej 15,3 DK - Copenhagen NV Denmark
Tel. (+45) 3531 0330
www.scanpublishing.dk
info@scanpublishing.dk
All rights reserved.

Text: Cristina Marques
Illustrations and graphic design:
Belli Studio, Gao Hanyu
Translation: Ruth Marschalek, Lissa Jensen

Printed in China
ISBN: 978 87 7247 183 9